CRAFT ATTACK!

NATURE CRAFTS

Annalees Lim

W
FRANKLIN WATTS
LONDON • SYDNEY

First published in 2014 by Franklin Watts

Copyright © 2014 Arcturus Publishing Limited

Franklin Watts
338 Euston Road
London NW1 3BH

Franklin Watts Australia
Level 17/207 Kent Street, Sydney NSW 2000

Produced by Arcturus Publishing Limited,
26/27 Bickels Yard, 151–153 Bermondsey Street, London SE1 3HA

The right of Annalees Lim to be identified as the author of this work
has been asserted by her in accordance with the Copyright,
Designs and Patents Act 1988.

Editors: Joe Harris and Sara Gerlings
Design: Elaine Wilkinson
Cover design: Elaine Wilkinson
Photography: Simon Pask

A CIP catalogue record for this book is available from the British Library.

Dewey Decimal Classification Number 745.5'9

ISBN 978 1 4451 2932 7

Printed in China

Franklin Watts is a division of Hachette Children's Books, an Hachette UK company.
www.hachette.co.uk

SL003836UK
Supplier 03, Date 0114, Print Run 3033

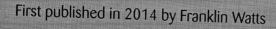

CONTENTS

GOING WILD WITH NATURE CRAFTS

When you next take a walk through a wood or a trip to the seaside, stop and look around you. There are so many interesting shapes and colours – even smells! You can use the objects that you find to create amazing craft projects.

Foraging Fun

It's possible to use natural objects in art and crafts all year round: from fresh flowers in spring, to shells on the beach in summer. In autumn, acorns and conkers are ready for discovering, and in winter you can collect small stones or make rubbings from the bark of trees.

Outdoor Inspiration

You don't have to travel very far to discover a whole world of interesting creatures and habitats. Even in the smallest of gardens you can find interesting objects for craft projects and inspiration from plants and animals.

Look Before You Touch

Remember that not everything you discover from your outdoor adventures can be collected, so ask an adult first if you're unsure. It's important to wash everything you find before you use it, to get rid of any small bugs or dirt.

A Bag or Basket

A top tip is always to carry a small bag or basket with you wherever you go. Plastic or canvas bags fold up really small and can be carried in pockets or rucksacks, so you will always be ready to collect craft materials, wherever you may be.

Pencils and Pens

It is a great idea to have a pot or pencil case full of different pens and pencils. Start with a nice sharp drawing pencil (HB is good), a set of colouring pencils and some felt-tip pens.

Scissors

Even though you can tear and rip paper, most of the time you will want to cut crisp lines. Always be careful when using scissors! If you need to cut tougher materials such as plastic, ask an adult to help.

PVA Glue

A crafts essential! This works well for sticking most things together.

Glue Sticks

These are quick and easy for sticking together pieces of paper.

Fabric Glue and Craft Glue

Fabric glue works well for sticking paper or card to (yes, you guessed it) fabric! Craft glue is useful if you need to stick on metal or plastic things (such as buttons or googly eyes).

WOODLAND PHOTO FRAME

Bring memories of outdoor fun back into your home with this woodland–inspired photo frame. You could use it to show off holiday snaps of your friends or family, or photographs of nature.

You will need

Cardboard
Twigs
Craft glue
Scissors
Ruler

1 Cut out two cardboard squares that measure roughly 15 x 15 cm (6 x 6 in). Cut out a smaller, 9 x 9-cm (3.5 x 3.5-in) square in the middle of one of the larger squares.

2 Cut out two cardboard rectangles that measure 1 x 15 cm (0.5 x 6 in) and another one that measures 1 x 13 cm (0.5 x 5 in). Then cut out a triangle about 15 cm (6 in) tall.

3 Snap the twigs into 6-cm (2.5-in) pieces and start gluing them onto your cardboard frame, using craft glue. Leave them to dry.

4 Turn the frame over so that the cardboard is facing you. Glue the two longest card pieces to either side of the frame using craft glue. Stick the shorter rectangle to another side (this will be the bottom). Then spread some more craft glue onto the card pieces you have just stuck down and stick the square card piece on top.

5 Make a fold near the top of the triangle. Put some glue on the point above the fold and stick it onto the back of your frame. Leave this to dry completely. Then stand up your frame, and slide a photograph inside.

PAINTED PEBBLE PLANT POT

By painting lots of pebbles different colours and gluing them in place, you can create funky pictures and patterns. This plant pot can live indoors on your windowsill, or outdoors in the garden.

You will need

- Oldy plant pot
- 3 plastic pots
- Poster paint and brushes
- Plastic sheet
- Pebbles or small stones
- Plastic fork
- PVA glue
- Plaster and a plastic
- Spreading tool (e.g. a plastic spoon)

1 Mix together an equal amount of paint and water in three plastic pots. Use three colours.

2 Pour in some of your pebbles or small stones and mix well until all of them are coated in the paint mixture.

3 Lift the pebbles out of each pot using a plastic fork, so that most of the paint mixture is strained away. Wash the fork between pots, so that you don't mix up the colours. Then leave the stones to dry on a plastic sheet.

4 Now coat your clay pot in a layer of plaster, using a plastic tool. Ask an adult to help you with the plastering, and carefully follow the instructions on the tin or bag.

6 Press your coloured pebbles into the wet plaster to make a pattern. Leave it to dry in a warm place. Coat your pot in a layer of PVA glue. This will seal it so that it can be used outside. Finally, paint around the top of your plant pot to complete your design.

You could also use painted pebbles to make mosaic artworks for your room. Just press them into a square of air-drying clay!

BUTTERFLY BUNTING

Brighten up your room with this brilliant decoration! The colourful pattern is made by rubbing leaves, then adding watercolour paints.

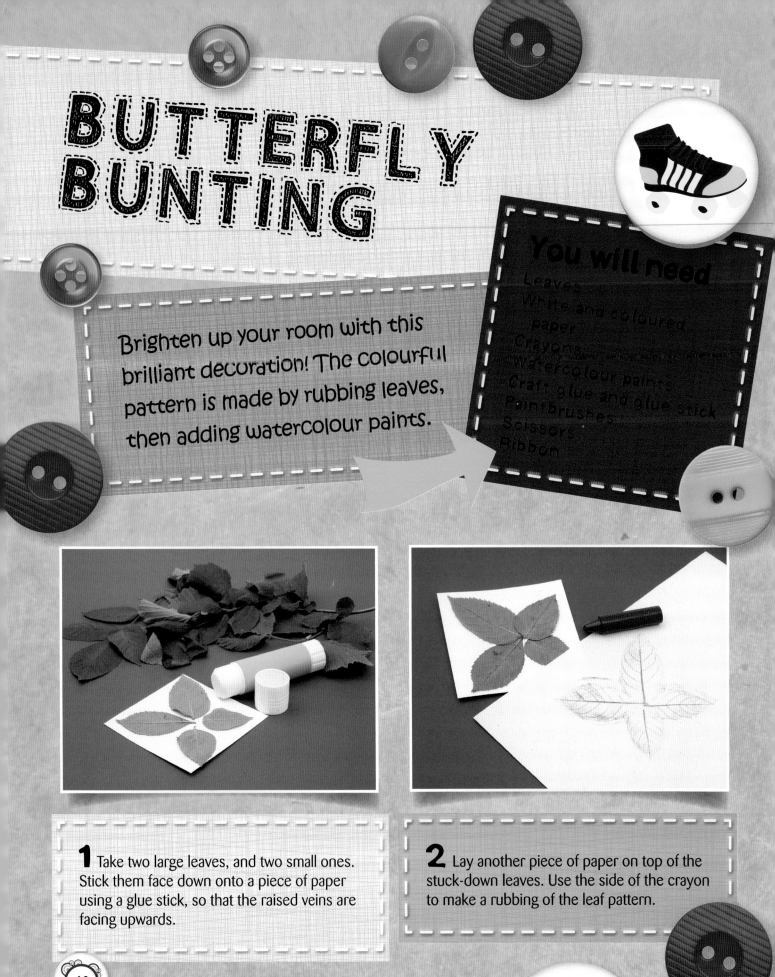

1 Take two large leaves, and two small ones. Stick them face down onto a piece of paper using a glue stick, so that the raised veins are facing upwards.

2 Lay another piece of paper on top of the stuck-down leaves. Use the side of the crayon to make a rubbing of the leaf pattern.

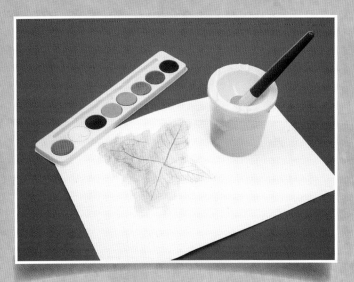

3 Paint a layer of watercolour paint over the top of the rubbing. Leave it to dry.

4 Cut around the leaf shape so it looks like a butterfly. Repeat steps 1–4 to make lots of different butterflies in lots of different colours.

5 Stick the butterflies onto a length of ribbon using craft glue.

6 Cut out the butterflies' body shape from coloured paper and stick it on with glue.

SAND ART

Sand is fun to play with when you're at the beach. But did you know you can also use it to create awesome art? Here's how you can make coloured sand and use it for fab decorations that will remind you of those dreamy days in the sun.

1 Pour some sand into five plastic pots. Add a few drops of food colouring to each pot so that you make five different colours of sand. Mix it well with the end of a paintbrush so that all the sand is coated with the colouring.

2 Spread the coloured sand onto a plastic sheet. This will help it to dry faster.

3 Using the funnel, pour the coloured sand into the glass bottle. You want to make a stripey pattern, so use one colour at a time.

4 Once you have filled the whole bottle, screw the lid back on. If your bottle does not have a lid, you can seal it with sticky tape instead.

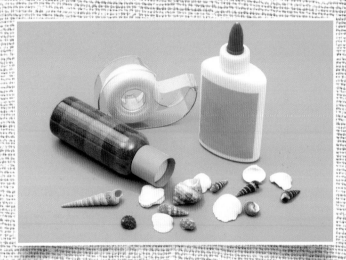

5 Wrap some coloured paper around the neck of the bottle and tape it in place. Stick on some seashells using PVA glue.

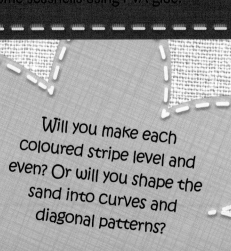

Will you make each coloured stripe level and even? Or will you shape the sand into curves and diagonal patterns?

SHELL CREATURE FRIDGE MAGNETS

Have you ever collected shells from the seaside? You can find them in many shapes and sizes. Here is the perfect craft for you to transform your shell collection into cute and crazy creatures!

You will need

Shells
Bowl, soap and sponge
Acrylic paint
Paintbrush
Craft glue
Googly eyes
Coloured card
Scissors
Magnets
Metallic pens

1 Use warm, soapy water and a soft sponge to clean all your shells well, making sure that they don't have any sand left on them.

2 Paint your shells in different colours using acrylic paint and leave to dry. You can also try painting some in different patterns such as stripes, dots or swirls.

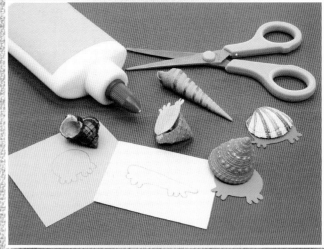

3 Add to your design using felt-tip pens. Metallic colours look especially good.

4 Cut out some feet from the coloured card using a pair of scissors. Then stick each of them onto the backs of the shells with craft glue.

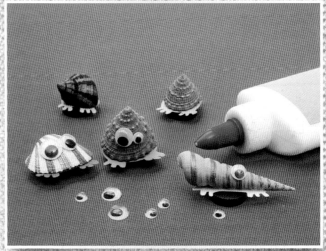

5 Stick a magnet onto the card on the back of each shell, using craft glue. Leave them to dry.

6 Stick one big googly eye and one small googly eye onto each shell using craft glue. Leave to dry.

PRESSED FLOWER COASTERS

Keep flowers looking bright and colourful by pressing them before they start to wilt. You can preserve them forever by turning them into classy coasters. These make a fantastic gift!

1 Sandwich your flowers between two sheets of kitchen towel and two heavy books. Leave them to dry out in a warm, dry place for a few weeks.

2 Cut out squares of coloured paper that are slightly smaller than your tiles. Stick them onto your tiles using some PVA glue.

3 Coat each tile in PVA glue and stick on your pressed flowers. You could also stick on leaf shapes cut from paper. Leave to dry.

4 Ask an adult to help you with this step. Give each tile a coat of acrylic sealer. Leave it to dry and then apply another coat.

5 Cut some squares of felt to the same size as your tiles. Stick the felt to the back of the tiles with fabric glue.

If your family are redecorating the house, you could make several tiles to decorate the bathroom or kitchen.

LEAFY BIRD MOBILE

You can find leaves all year round, but their colours will depend on the season. Make use of this great natural craft material by creating a fun mobile.

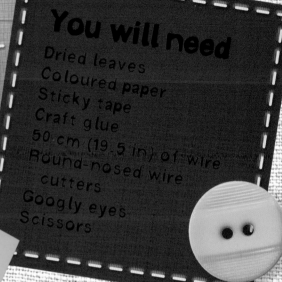

You will need
Dried leaves
Coloured paper
Sticky tape
Craft glue
50 cm (19.5 in) of wire
Round-nosed wire cutters
Googly eyes
Scissors

1 You will need eight big leaves and eight small leaves to make eight birds. Stick all the leaves onto coloured paper using sticky tape. Make sure you cover the whole leaf with tape.

2 Cut around each leaf shape with your scissors, making sure you leave a 0.5-cm (0.2-in) border of coloured paper.

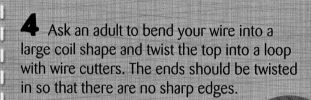

3 Stick a small leaf to a bigger leaf using sticky tape, to make a body and wing. Add a paper triangle for a beak, and another piece of paper for a tail. Finally, stick on a googly eye with craft glue. Do this eight times.

4 Ask an adult to bend your wire into a large coil shape and twist the top into a loop with wire cutters. The ends should be twisted in so that there are no sharp edges.

5 Stick the birds to the outside of the coil using more sticky tape. Make them look as though they are flying together!

6 Add some paper leaf shapes to the coil and finish the mobile by attaching some ribbon to the top so you can hang it up.

SEED MOSAIC

All plants come from seeds, so there is plenty of choice when it comes to making this craft! We have used black poppy seeds, but you could try using sunflower seeds, pumpkin seeds or even mixed bird seeds!

You will need

Seeds
PVA glue
Card
Scissors
Ruler
Black marker pen
Poster paints
Paintbrush

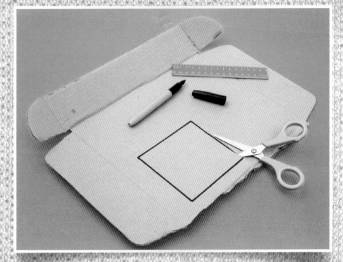

1 Measure and cut out a 15 x 15-cm (6 x 6-in) square of card.

2 Draw a pattern on the card using a black marker pen.

3 Cut a petal shape into the top of each piece of folded tissue paper. Open it up to reveal a flower! Place each white flower on top of a pink flower and twist them at the centre to hold them together.

4 Stick the flowers onto your tree branch with PVA glue and repeat until you have covered the whole branch.

5 Fill the base with the pebbles. As a finishing touch, you could decorate your blossom tree with sparkly sequins.

PEBBLE ZOO

Collect stones of different sizes and shapes to make these cute creatures. You could use them as paperweights, bookends or decorations for your room.

1 Stick a medium-sized stone to a large stone using craft glue, to make a head and body for your creature. Then glue four smaller stones to the large stone to make some legs.

2 Repeat step 1 twice. To make the zebra, stick another small stone onto the front of the medium stone. This will be the muzzle.

3 Paint the animals using acrylic paint. Use yellow for the lion, white for the zebra and grey for the elephant.

4 Cut out an elephant's ears, trunk and tail from blue felt. Cut out a lion's mane, tail and nose from orange felt. Cut out a zebra's stripes, mane and tail from black felt.

5 Stick the felt shapes onto the animals with fabric glue. Draw more details onto the animals using a black marker pen and finish them off by sticking on googly eyes with craft glue.

BRILLIANT BIRD BOX

Birds usually make their nests by collecting twigs. You can make a nifty bird box by collecting twigs yourself! This will look great in any garden. Why not use seeds to tempt some visitors inside?

You will need
- Lots of twigs
- Secateurs
- Ruler
- Craft glue
- Masking tape

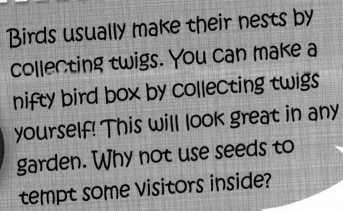

1 Ask an adult to help you cut down your twigs so that they are all 10 cm (4 in) long. You will need to use secateurs for this.

2 Lay enough sticks next to each other to make a 10 x 10-cm (4 in x 4-in) square. Do this six times.

3 Glue two sticks across each square with craft glue so that they hold the twigs together. Now leave everything to dry completely.

4 Glue the six squares together to form a house shape with a floor, three walls and a pointed roof. While the craft glue is drying, hold everything in place with masking tape.

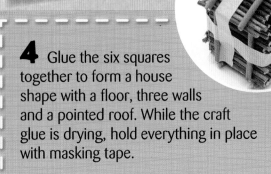

5 Remove all the masking tape when the bird box has fully dried.

PINE CONE FIELD MOUSE

Pine cones are plentiful in autumn. Why not turn one into a cute little field mouse?

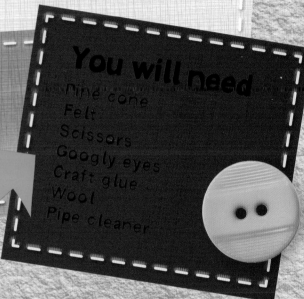

You will need
- Pine cone
- Felt
- Scissors
- Googly eyes
- Craft glue
- Wool
- Pipe cleaner

1 Cut out some round ears, an oval face, two arms and some feet from brown felt. Cut out smaller ear shapes and a nose from pink felt.

2 Stick together the pink and brown parts of the ears with craft glue. Then glue all the felt shapes except the nose to the pine cone.

3 Using the craft glue, stick some googly eyes to the face.

4 Cut some brown wool into short lengths to make the whiskers. Stick them just under the mouse's eyes with craft glue. Glue the nose on top of the whiskers.

5 Stick the pipe cleaner tail to the back of the pine cone and curl it slightly.

LAVENDER HAND WARMERS

Dried lavender smells great, and you can use it to stuff all sorts of things – such as this heart-shaped strawberry! You will need to ask an adult for help with the sewing.

You will need

- Red and green cotton fabric
- Rice
- Dried lavender
- Large cup or bowl
- Scissors
- Needle and white thread
- Black marker

1 Fill a large cup or bowl two thirds of the way up with rice, then fill it to the top with dried lavender. Mix them together.

2 Cut out a heart shape from red fabric measuring about 12 cm (4.7 in) across . Trace around it with a marker, then cut out another identical shape.

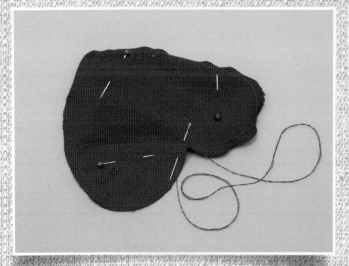

3 Carefully sew the two hearts together around the edge, making sure you leave a small 5-cm (2-in) gap somewhere.

4 Turn the heart inside out to hide the stitching. Fill it with rice mixture. Then sew up the gap to make sure nothing spills out.

5 Cut out two stalk shapes from green fabric and sew them onto each side of the strawberry. Sew on white seed shapes using your white cotton thread. Do this on both sides.

Now pop the bag into the microwave for 10 seconds to warm it up. The smell of lavender is very relaxing, and warmth can help to relieve aches and pains.

GLOSSARY

bonsai An ornamental, miniature tree, artifically prevented from growing to its full size.

bunting A traditional decoration made from triangles of material attached to a length of string.

forage To search over a large area.

mosaic A piece of art created by arranging small pieces of hard, coloured material (such as stones, tiles or glass) to make a picture.

raffia A ribbon-like fibre made from palm leaves.

wilt (plants) To become limp due to disease, heat or lack of water.

FURTHER READING

Find It, Make It: Outdoor Green Crafts for Children by Clare Youngs (CUCO Books, 2011)

Fun with Nature by Annalees Lim (Wayland, 2013)

Garden Crafts for Children by Dawn Isaac (CICO Books, 2012)

Make It Wild!: 101 Things to Make and Do Outdoors by Fiona Danks (Frances Lincoln, 2010)

WEBSITES

kids.nationalgeographic.co.uk/kids/activities/crafts/
Crafts inspired by nature

tlc.howstuffworks.com/family/nature-crafts.htm-
Heaps of craft ideas using natural resources

www.busybeekidscrafts.com/Outdoor-Crafts.html
Ideas for using the nature around you to make crafts

INDEX

SERIES CONTENTS